DIETICIANS

PEOPLE WHO CARE FOR OUR HEALTH

Robert James

The Rourke Book Co., Inc.
Vero Beach, Florida 32964

Acknowledgments
The author thanks Mercy Center, Aurora, IL, for its cooperation in
the publication of this book.

Library of Congress Cataloging-in-Publication Data

James, Robert, 1942-
    Dieticians / by Robert James.
      p. cm. — (People who care for our health)
    Includes index.
    Summary: Describes what dieticians do, where they work, and
how they train for their jobs.
    ISBN 1-55916-168-X
    1. Dietetics—Vocational guidance—Juvenile literature.
[1. Dietetics—Vocational guidance. 2. Vocational guidance.
3. Occupations.]
I. Title II. Series: James, Robert, 1942- People who care for our
health
RM217.J35 1995
613'.2'023—dc20   95–18938
                                          CIP
                                          AC

Printed in the USA

TABLE OF CONTENTS

DIETICIANS

Dieticians are health care **professionals** (pro FESH un ulz) who know a lot about food. That doesn't mean they're big eaters or cooks. Instead, dieticians are experts in **nutrition** (NU trish un).

Nutrition is all about how food is used by the human body and how the body can best be nourished.

Dieticians help people learn which foods to eat and when to eat them. They work especially with people who need to make changes in their diet—the foods they normally eat.

Dieticians are experts in the ways that the human body uses food

STUDYING NUTRITION

Dieticians closely watch the results of scientific studies about food. They watch for changes in laws that may affect how foods are grown, treated, or processed. Dieticians also study diseases caused by poor diets.

By keeping up with new information about food, dieticians can better perform other parts of their job. One other part of that job is **counseling** (KOWN sel ing).

Dieticians stay in touch with how farmers grow and fertilize food

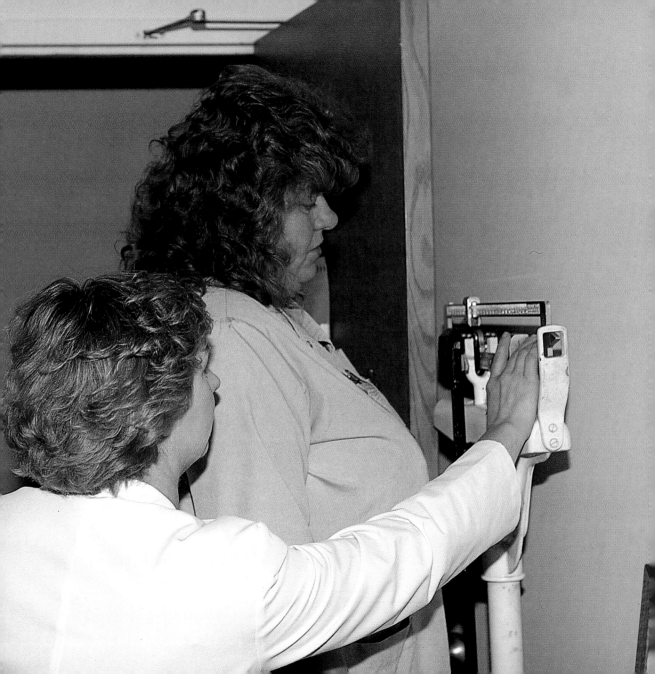

COUNSELING

As counselors, dieticians work closely with one patient at a time. The dietician studies the problem and discusses it with the patient. The dietician may then suggest a change in the patient's diet.

A dietician's patients are often people who have a disease, such as diabetes or cancer. Many other patients have had heart attacks. Some patients are under- or overweight and lacking the proper **nutrients** (NU tree nts).

Dieticians work closely with their patients

NUTRIENTS

All food is not equal. Foods do not taste the same. We learn that at an early age. More important, though, is the fact that the substances in some foods are much better for us than others. These "good" substances are called nutrients.

Everyone who wants to be healthy needs the proper amount of nutrients.

Dieticians teach small groups about good nutrition and new findings about nutrition

With a meat thermometer, a hospital dietician checks to see if the chicken is properly cooked

A dietician highlights diet "do's and don'ts" with a hospital patient

USING NUTRIENTS

Part of a dietician's job is to decide what amount of each nutrient a person needs.

Because each person is different, his or her nutrient need is different from the next person's.

Nutrients are used by the body to build and strengthen flesh and bone. They keep the body's systems working right. Nutrients are also the body's jet fuel—its source of energy.

A dietician tries to find the correct balance of nutrients for each patient

A BALANCED DIET

Dieticians teach people that they should have a balanced diet. That means a diet with the proper amount of nutrients from each of five nutrient groups—carbohydrates, fats, proteins, minerals, and vitamins.

Each group provides the body with something good. Carbohydrates, for example, give us energy. But too much of a nutrient—fat, perhaps—can be as bad as too little.

A dietician makes sure that the hospital kitchen prepares a balanced menu

FOOD GROUPS

Our bodies work and build from the nutrients in the foods we eat. Food comes in four basic groups —milk products, meat and eggs, bread and cereals, and vegetables and fruits.

A diet that includes food from all groups—in the correct amounts—is the path to good nutrition.

A dietician helps people to understand the value of good nutrition and how to achieve it.

Fresh vegetables mean good nutrition for people as well as Brer Rabbit

WHERE DIETICIANS WORK

Dieticians work in nursing homes for elderly people, **clinics** (KLIN ihks), and some health clubs. They also work for large companies, in private offices of their own, and in hospitals.

Hospital dieticians may counsel patients in the patient's room or in the dietician's office. Hospital dieticians also plan the hospital's meals for its patients.

Dieticians sometimes work with school and community groups and with restaurant owners.

A hospital dietician checks the food line for cleanliness and variety

BECOMING A DIETICIAN

Dieticians are highly trained. A dietician must have a four-year college degree in nutrition. Many dieticians continue their education and earn a Master's degree.

A dietician must also serve an **internship** (IN turn ship) before working alone. An intern dietician works for several months under the direction of an experienced dietician.

Glossary

clinic (KLIN ihk) — a place, usually with several doctors, for treating large numbers of patients who don't need overnight care

counseling (KOWN sel ing) — the act of offering helpful advice and information

internship (IN turn ship) — a trial period during which an inexperienced person works with an experienced person on a job

nutrient (NU tree nt) — a body-building ingredient in food; any one of the five groups of nutrients

nutrition (NU trish un) — the ways that the body uses food; the nourishing of the body by healthy foods

professional (pro FESH un ul) — one who is highly trained, highly skilled, and paid for his or her work

INDEX